T0114855

YOUR MAMA WAS WRONG

by

Dennis O. Evans

YOUR MAMA WAS WRONG

BY

DENNIS O. EVANS

Order this book online at www.trafford.com
or email orders@trafford.com

Most Trafford titles are also available at major online book retailers.

Print information available on the last page.

ISBN: 978-1-4120-0570-8 (sc)
ISBN: 978-1-4122-1353-0 (e)

Trafford rev. 02/10/2020

Trafford
PUBLISHING® www.trafford.com
North America & international
toll-free: 1 888 232 4444 (USA & Canada)
fax: 812 355 4082

Dedication

This book is dedicated to the many friends and family members who listened to my controversial views. I especially remember my friend Henrique Fritt who challenged me to read and search for truth. I dedicate this book also to my mother Lola Moss Evans, who was the first to hear me challenge the status quo-her. Finally, I want to dedicate this book to my daughter Roberta Denyce Joseph and her husband Mark and my son Dennis O. Evans Jr.

Acknowledgments

I owe thanks to my wife, Mary, who provided a pleasant home atmosphere that enabled me to think and to write. My wife's daughters, Cassandra Alexander and Barbara Davis helped with computer skills as did my friends Rusty and Barbara McCellan.

.

TABLE OF CONTENTS

Forward

"Your Mama Was Wrong"

This book is not literally about our mamas being wrong. It is about the wrong things that society in general taught us. However, our parents were influenced by society. Many untruths have been believed for hundreds of years. Over the years these beliefs became accepted as facts.

This book is about some of the myths that we have accepted as true but are in fact, not true or half-true. When we uncover these myths we sometimes come face to face with a reality that is the exact opposite of what we have been taught. This reality can bring us into direct conflict with society. We may be ridiculed, criticized, or physically attacked. There will be more questions raised than answered.

Change makes some people uncomfortable. They will do whatever they can to resist change. Laws are sometimes passed in order to maintain the status quo and avoid the emotional pain of change.

Some of what you read may shock you. Some of it may anger you. Some of it may make you laugh. I hope all of it will cause you to think about why you believe what you believe. The essays in this book are not meant to change your opinion but are meant to encourage you to challenge long held traditions. It is hoped that this book will cause you to think about why you believe what you believe. You might disagree with what you read just because it is different from what you have been taught.

Lying is OK

Your mama was wrong when she told you to never tell a lie. She should have told you to never tell a lie on someone. There are times when it can be very dangerous to tell the truth. One of the Ten Commandments says "Thou shalt not bare false witness against thy neighbor." (Exodus 20:16.) It means don't lie on your neighbor. Who is your neighbor? Your neighbor is anyone who needs your help or protection. You have no obligation to tell the truth to those who would use it to hurt you or others.

When the runaway slaves were being hidden in the "Underground Railroad," it would have been dangerous to them if the truth about where they were hiding had been told. People lied in order to protect and help them. If POWs were planning an escape, it would be dangerous if someone in the group was committed to always telling the truth. When asked, he or she would tell the guards the truth. There is no obligation to tell the truth to the enemy.

There are people who are not your neighbors or your enemies. They do not need your help or protection. A lie to them has little or no meaning. When your mama does not want to talk to someone and she says " Tell them I am not home," it is a lie that has little or no consequences. It is not wrong because it is not against anyone.

There are also times when your mama is not home and someone calls. You should lie and say she is not available. That is somewhat truthful. If she is not home she is not available. It is also a little deceptive. Some people, who mean you no good will call just to see if you are alone. You are under no obligation to tell the truth to these people. Here again telling the truth could be dangerous.

Lying seems to be a basic part of our culture. Even clothes can be used for deception. Clothes are sometimes used to give an impression that is not an accurate picture of us. The clothes reflect who we want people to think we are, not who we really are. The same can be said of makeup and deodorant. There is nothing wrong with these deceptions as long as they are not used to hurt or harm someone.

In almost all of our team sports some type of deception is used in order to win. It is part of the game. We do not think of the tricks that we play on our opponents as lies but they are. In literature we call books that are not true fiction. Something that is not true is a lie. Fiction covers everything from children's stories to major motion pictures. In most of our motion pictures the actors pretend to be someone else. In other words, they lie. The best liars become stars.

Money

Your mama was wrong when she told you that " Money will not make you happy." She should have told you that the" lack of money will make you sad." People are proud of quoting the words "The love of money is the root of all evil." (1Tim 6:10). They fail to point out the fact that it says the **LOVE** of money "is the root of all evil." They also conveniently forget to quote the words "money answereth all things". (Eccl. 10:19).

I have yet to see people sad or angry because they received some money, but I have seen many people who were happy with smiling faces from ear to ear when they received some money. Money can get you all the things that you need and a lot of what you want. I said a lot of what you want because one of the things you will always want is more money. Needs are limited to air, water, food and shelter. Wants are unlimited. Take a look around and see how many smiling, happy faces are on people who are pushing shopping carts and collecting cans for a living! How many homeless, hungry people have big smiles on their faces? But some say the lack of money is not their problem but the lack of skills and motivation. But I say skills, education and motivation will help them solve their real problem, which is "lack of money." In the end it is about money. " Money answerth all things." (Eccl 10:19)

When my daughter graduated from college there was a big smile on her face. When she got that big paying job her smile was even bigger. O, sure, there will be times in life when you will get knocked down but it is nice to have a cushion of money to fall on. Money can help you get through the sad times, but the lack of money can make the sad times even worst.

Yes, your mama was wrong when she said that money will not make you happy because she should have added that the lack of money can make sad times bad times. Money can not make you happy but it will give you the freedom to do the things that will make you happy.

The desire to accumulate wealth is a natural inborn human trait. It comes from God." It is He that giveth thee power to get wealth." (Deut 8:18).

People with a lot of money have many friends. (People who know them) People with very little money have very few friends. "Wealth maketh many friends." (Prov.19:4). Many so -called friends of the rich will steal from them, but the friends of the poor will steal from them also. The friends of the rich will steal some of what he has but the friends of the poor will steal everything and leave him even poorer. If a rich man has three houses and one of them burns down, it is not the same as a poor man with one house that burns to the ground. Limited resources make limited choices. Money gives you freedom. It enables you to help others. This is where real happiness is found.

Who's Your Daddy?

This chapter will upset many of us. It will come as a big shock to the vast majority of us, but the truth is that the only one of us who knows for a fact who his or her father is, is the one with DNA proof. We know what our mothers told us. But no matter how much we love and believe them, their word is not scientific fact. We can holler and scream that our mothers will not lie to us but that will not change a lie into the truth. A fact is a fact regardless of how we feel about it.

I suspect that there are millions of people who have not been told the truth about their paternity. For some, even the mothers may not know. They may have been with more than one person in the same time frame. For others, they may have deliberately lied in order to protect their families or reputations. There have been cases where the mother did not know that the child she was raising was not hers because the hospital made a mistake and switched babies at birth. I wonder how many times has this mistake been made but never became news?

Every child born, within or without a marriage, should be given both a birth certificate and a DNA certificate. If such a requirement became the law, there would be a lot of messed up families. Many could not deal with the truth. Long past affairs would be discovered. Some may find out that they are heirs to great fortunes. Others may end up being disinherited. It would create quite a disturbance.

It is my conclusion that if a parent will lie about anything he or she, will lie about paternity. Your mama may be the best mother in the world and may love you with all of her heart and may even sacrifice her life for you, but concerning your paternity she will not tell you the truth. She may think that it's for your protection but in really it is for her reputation.

I believe that every child has the right to know his or her paternity. What sense does it make for everyone except you to know whom your father is? No individual or institution should know more about you than you know about yourself. Every individual has the right to keep his or her sex life private. But when there is a child involved the child's right to know his or her paternity overrules the parent's right to privacy.

Because many parents cannot bring themselves to the point of asking for a DNA test, it should be automatically done. People will object because they do not want their private sex lives made public. Why would anyone object to a child knowing who his or her parent is? Of course women could end up being divorced and men could end up paying child support for children outside of the marriage. The knowledge that all babies will be tested for paternity will cause people to think long and hard before having an affair involving unprotected sexual intercourse. Those who are unable to have children or who are past childbearing age will have other concerns.

Like any new revolutionary concept, it will cause social instability in the beginning, but after people get use to it, they will come to appreciate the peace that honesty and truthfulness can bring. It is not easy living with the fear that others will find out their secret. A secret, however, is something that only one person knows. If one other person knows, it is not a secret. There is no way of knowing how many people the other person has told. When there has been sex with another person, then the other person shares the knowledge. If a baby is conceived while having sex with more than one person, then a DNA test could be used to determine the paternity. However a DNA test is not needed if the baby's blood type is "AB" and the father's blood type is "O". It is impossible for a father with type "O" blood to be the parent of a baby with "AB" blood. He can be the parent of a baby with blood type "O", "A", "B", but not "AB". Many men with "O" blood never question the fact that the baby with "AB" blood can not be theirs. They may be unaware of the relationship between blood type and paternity. The mother, under the pretense of protecting her child, will lie about her sex life. Others may know the secret, but for fear of hurting her feelings will not tell. She may go to her grave believing that nobody knows. In fact, the mother may not know who the father of her child is. She may hope and believe that the child is her husband's, when in reality, only a DNA test or some other paternity test would reveal the truth. She knows that there is a possibility that the child might not be her husband's. Many couples would be shocked to learn the true identity of their children. It should not be surprising if parents become angry and upset when children asked for a DNA test. Some would be afraid of what the results might reveal. The fear that a secret might be revealed can make life miserable. According to available information, the effort of trying to keep something secret can cause stress and can be very unhealthy. The stress can lower the immune system and make individuals subject to various diseases. To prevent this from happening, parents should not keep paternity secrets from their children. Finally, for medically reasons, children may need to know who their biological parent is.

At what time or age should a child be told about his or her paternity? There is no set time or age. Parents should be totally honest with the child from the very beginning. It will be difficult to tell a mature child the truth about his or her paternity but it must be done. There can be no justification for keeping from a person the truth about his or her paternity.

Nudity

Your mama was wrong about nudity. When people hear that someone is a nudist they often say, "Why would anyone want to walk around nude?" But that is the wrong question. The question should be "Why do people wear clothes anyway?" Adam and Eve were created nude and everyone who has entered this world since them has entered it nude. Adam and Eve were nude and were not ashamed. Babies are nude and are not ashamed. Shame is not natural it must be learned. In fact, there seems to be a natural desire for humans to wear as few clothes as possible. If nudity is natural because we are born nude, does this mean that wearing clothes is unnatural?

When God first created man there were seven things declared very good. They were marriage, work, equality, free will, vegetarianism, the Sabbath, and nudity, Genesis 2 and 3. After they sinned it is taught that six of these seven remained good but nudity became bad. It is believed that Adam and Eve covered their nude bodies because of shame. In other words, shame for nudity was the result of sin.

The question to be considered is could there have been another reason? The text says " the eyes of them both were opened, and they knew that they were naked" (Gen. 3:7). It does not say that they were shame of being naked just that they knew that they were naked. Adam later tells God "I was afraid, because I was naked." (Gen. 3:10) What was there about being naked that caused him to fear? Was he afraid that God who had made him naked would see him naked? It does not say. It only says that he was afraid because he was naked. It does not say that he was ashamed. He was not aware of his nudity until after his sin when he knew that he was naked. I suggest that he became aware of his nudity when he felt the discomfort of cold air for the first time on his skin. This told him that he was now subject to death. This is what caused his fear. He covered himself for protection from the cold air. The text says he heard God in the "cool of the day". (Genesis 3:8) For better protection God made him a garment of skins. Did God turn his back while Adam changed clothes?

The idea that Adam and Eve put on clothes for protection is the reason that historians say man first wore clothes. Compton's Encyclopedia says "one reason man first wore clothing was for protection." V.5.p. 505. World Book Encyclopedia says, "Early people may have worn clothes to protect themselves." Ibid...4cp .686. The conservative religious writer E.G. White, in commenting on Genesis wrote, "The atmosphere once so mild and uniform in temperature, was now subject to marked changes, and the Lord mercifully provided them with garments of skins as a protection from the cold" (Patriarchs and Prophets p.56). Apparently, this was the view of the early Christian Church because nude mixed bathing was a common and popular activity by Christian men and women in the spas of Rome until around 400 AD. Paintings in baptisteries of some early Christian Churches show a nude Christ being baptized. The church conducted all baptisms in the nude until around 1500. Hans Memling clearly showed a nude baptism in his 1489 painting " The Arrival in Rome." The nudity was symbolic of the innocence of a newborn baby. The idea of wearing clothes for concealment did not become universally accepted until after 1500 AD. The historian Norbert Elias in writing about Europe says, " Up until the sixteenth century, the sight of total nudity was an everyday rule." The Civilizing Process p.164

The explorer, Captain Cook, in his travels, encountered entire naked cultures. Many of these cultures changed after the arrival of the European and Puritan Missionaries. Partial nudity was also common among the native Indians. Many of the American slaves were nude or partially nude. Most of our negative attitudes about nudity came from the self-appointed reformer Anthony Comstock of the 1870s. We get our word "comstockery" from his name. He lobbied against what he thought was obscene material. Contraception, abortion, and nudity were his special targets. He was so effective in getting laws passed that the subject of contraception became unmentionable-even in medical textbooks. It was during this period that nudity became associated with sex and obscenity. Nudity, which had been common in the movies and the arts, disappeared and did not reappear until the late 50s and early 60s. With the reappearance of nudity came a new attitude. Nudity became identified with sex and obscenity. All nudity was considered sexual and dirty. To most people there was no such thing as non-sexual nudity. Gymnophobia, or fear of nudity, became fixed.

Many celebrities are so fearful of being photographed in the nude that they go to extreme measures to protect their privacy. A nude picture of a celebrity is very valuable. Photographers go to great lengths to obtain one. However, the value of the photograph is based upon how special the celebrity thinks seeing him or her in the nude is. The more difficult it is to obtain the greater its value. Look at what happens to the value of a celebrity's nude photo once she (it is usually a she) is in Playboy. Nude pictures of her no longer have commercial value. When a celebrity thinks and acts like a nude photo of her is something special it becomes special. Those who are harassed are those who make a big deal out of it.

The debate over the good and bad about nudity has a long history. Two thousand years before Christ, Socrates wrote that if women want to be equal they should strip naked and exercise together with Greek men. Female modesty separates the sexes. As long as females claim that their bodies are special and should be covered modestly, they cannot be equal. Our society believes that a woman should cover her top whether her breasts are small or large. Even little girls are expected to cover their breasts. Actually it is not the breasts that society wants covered but the nipples. Many of the dress styles of today show most of the breasts. Low cut dresses are common. These dresses show almost all of the breasts. Some of the bikini bathing suits cover only the nipples. Our society considers it to be immodest for a woman to show her nipples. It is difficult to understand why because there is virtually no difference between the nipples of a man and the nipples of a woman. If a woman covers all of her breasts but reveals her nipples she will be considered more immodest than a woman who reveals her entire breasts but covers her nipples. This objection to the sight of nipples is so unreasonable that many in society object to the innocent sight of a woman nursing her baby.

Society's objection to nudity has no reasonable basis. Because of the anatomical location of the anus and vagina, it would be impossible to see them even if the woman was naked. A thong bikini does not cover the anus. The anus is anatomically hidden. Likewise, the pubic hair does not cover the vagina. The vagina is also anatomically hidden.

The objection to nudity is often based upon religious and cultural beliefs. History has shown that religions and cultures have constantly changed what they have considered immodest. Some years ago it was considered immodest for a woman to show her ankles in public. Covering the genitals in public may be modest, however, the breasts and nipples are not genitals. The artist Michelangelo, commenting on the beauty of nudity, said, "What spirit is so empty and blind, that it cannot grasp the fact that the human foot is more noble that the shoe and the human skin more beautiful than the garment with which it is clothed?" Mark Twain wrote, "Adam and Eve entered the world naked and unashamed- naked and pure minded, and no descendant of theirs has ever entered it otherwise. All have entered it naked, unashamed, and clean in mind. They entered it modest. They had to acquire immodesty in the soiled mind. There was no other way to get it...The convention mis-called ' modesty ' has no standard, and cannot have one, because it is opposed to nature and reason and is therefore an artificiality and subject to anyone's whim-anyone's diseased caprice." Letters from the Earth.

The psychologist Abraham Maslow wrote "I have the feeling that a spread of nudism would be a step in the direction of greater ease and equality for men and women, for many reasons. First of all, it would make them less strange to each other; there would be less sexual exploring merely for the sake of curiosity. It seem to me also that such love as would emerge would be more on the social and emotional side than on the purely physical side." The Right to be Human, pg. 135, Ed Hoffman. Finally, we have a man with the opposite view not only on nudity but also just about everything. He said, "The total exposure of the human body is undignified as well as an error of taste." Adolph Hitler "Beyond Nakedness" p.89 by Paul Ableman. What would Hitler know about human dignity and taste?

One final thought on the subject of nudity. Is the basis for the phobia about nudity based on religious or cultural beliefs? There seem to be some racism involved. If it is morally wrong for a woman to be topless, why is there no objection when a minority from a third world country is shown topless? Minority women are women too. Why is it all right to show them nude on TV and in magazines but wrong to show a white woman? It is common to see topless minority women on national TV. Recently, in a movie on national television, African women were dancing topless. A white woman joined in the dancing, however, she never removed her top. If the objection to nudity is based upon morality then black nudity should be just as wrong as white nudity. This is not the case. In our schools there are national magazines which routinely show pictures of nude women from third world countries. The message given to children is that minority women from third world countries are not human. In our society morality does not apply to animals or third world people.

Those who think that they would be shocked at a nudist resort are really shocked at the thought of being at a nudist resort. Just the word "nude" shocks many people. It's the thought that shocks them. The fear of being nude is located only in their minds. It is a phobia. It is the fear of something that is relatively harmless. The fear is real but the thing feared is imagined. In society today, a nude picture is often considered dirty. A person who is shocked at the sight of nudity is said to be a person with a clean mind. The truth is that a person who is shocked at the sight of nudity has a dirty mind. The psychologist A.S. Neill wrote, "A clean mind is one that cannot be shocked. To be shocked is to show that you have repressions that make you interested in what shocks you." (Summerhill p. 351). When people visit a nudist resort they are shocked at not being shocked. They find themselves feeling safe among entirely nude families where their little girls play around totally nude men. Where else on earth can this take place? Church groups cannot claim such safety. (No concealed weapons!) The nudist resort reflects the way the world would have been if there had not been sin. I wonder if the people on other worlds are nude? This fear of nudity runs so deep that the aliens in our science fiction movies have on clothes.. What is the basis for their objection to nudity?

Why did the apes in the movie "Planet of the Apes" have on clothes? Did they buy the clothes at a major department store on their planet? Why do we think the fear of nudity is universal?

People who have a fear of being seen nude or seeing someone nude are mentally ill. The fear of something that is relatively harmless is a phobia. A phobia is a type of mental illness. This type of mental illness is so common that it is considered normal to have a fear of nudity. Those who have overcome this phobia are called abnormal. We seem to have come to a time when what is good is called bad and what is bad is called good.

Violent Criminals

Your mama was wrong about crime and punishment. Our society seems to be at an impasse when it comes to crime and punishment. Violent criminals do their crimes, do their time, get out and repeat their crimes. In other words, most violent criminals become repeat offenders.

Our criminal justice system should punish the criminal for the crime, protect society from the career criminal, and give the criminal an opportunity to become a productive citizen. Unfortunately there is nothing in our system today that will do all three. Some states use the death penalty to punish violent criminals. It however, is flawed. It does not punish the criminal. A live person can be punished but a dead person cannot. A criminal may fear death but as far as we know he doesn't feel death. The death penalty punishes the living for it causes the living to feel the pain of separation and loss. The dead criminal will not miss the hugs, kisses, and sounds of his loved ones. The relatives and friends who are left behind are the ones who will feel the loss.

A criminal kills a mother's son and she suffers grief over the loss of her son. The state then kills the criminal and his mother then feels the loss of her son. We have two mothers suffering grief over the loss of their sons. We call this justice! Punishing the innocent is nothing but cruel. While it is true that the death penalty prevents repeat crimes it does not punish the criminal and it does not give him the opportunity to become a productive citizen of society.

What, then, is the solution? Is there something that society can do to punish the criminal, protect society, and rehabilitate the criminal? The answer is yes! Rapists, murderers, abusers, and molesters all have one thing in common. Eliminate that one thing and their life of crime will end.

The solution may sound cruel and barbaric at first but if it is examined closely it will be recognized as the solution to our violent crime problem. Violent criminals have one thing in common- eyesight. They must be able to see in order to commit their crimes. Without eyesight it would be impossible for them to repeat their crimes Blindness will solve the violent crime problem. Blindness will (1) Punish the criminal, (2) Protect society from repeat offenders and (3) Provide an opportunity for the criminal to become a productive citizen of society. How many children would be alive today if child molesters were blinded on their first offense? Convicted child molesters who have been released from prison, still express an uncontrollable desire to continue to molest. However, if they could not see, they would be unable to fulfill their desire. A blind registered sex offender would be unable to continue his life of crime. Those who have been raped or abused and now live in fear after their attacker has been released would have no concern knowing that their attacker could not see. The blind criminals would live in fear of those whom they had attacked.

Before rejecting this solution as cruel, consider the fact that we can now make blindness temporary or permanent. Because of advances in medical science we now have the ability to sentence a criminal to a set period of blindness or permanent blindness. Blindness is much more humane that the death penalty. A blind criminal could still work, get married, and become a productive citizen. (Blindness would be a good solution for people with multiple drunk driving convictions.)

The violent criminal's mother is not punished with the loss of her son, but the criminal is punished with the loss of his sight. If later he is found not guilty, his sight can be restored but if he is given the death penalty, his life can not be restored. The cost of caring for a blind criminal who is released from prison would be far less than caring for a criminal in prison. In fact, I am not sure that society owes the violent criminal anything. As things are now, victims, through taxes, help to care for the attacker. That is cruel!

Should a rape victim be forced to care for the rapist through taxes? Again, that is what can be called cruel!

Gambling

Your mama was wrong about gambling. All people gamble. Almost everything people do is a gamble. They may gamble with their money or they may gamble with their lives. Many people are in denial about gambling. In fact, they will become angry if it is implied that they gamble. Nevertheless whenever a decision is made that involves winning or losing, it is a gamble. Most think that only gambling with money is wrong Gambling is not wrong, it is natural. What is wrong is betting against the odds or betting when there is little or no chance of winning.

Everyone agrees that playing slot machines in a casino is gambling. It is believed that gambling when there is such a small chance of winning is throwing money away. Few, however, will call being overweight gambling. But being overweight is gambling. It is betting that one can be overweight and still be healthy. Gambling in a casino will cost you your money. Gambling with your health will cost you your life. What is more important- your life or your money?

Some people who smoke and gamble with their health think that people who gamble in a casino are immoral. To them, gambling with their money is worst than gambling with their lives. People who drop out of school are gambling that they can be successful without an education. They are betting against the odds. People who do not exercise are betting that they can be healthy without regular exercise. They too, are betting against the odds. Those who marry when there are major differences in cultures, values, and ages, are betting against the odds. They are betting with their lives and the future lives of their children. Those who live without insurance are gambling that they want need it. If they lose this bet they will find

25

themselves in a very bad way. It can be financially devastating. Those who go out in the sun without protection are gambling. Those who do not wear seatbelts are gambling. Those who drive cars with defective brakes and tires are gambling. A few years ago a bulletin board read "If you gamble when you drive, you bet your life." Those who would never think of gambling in a casino, constantly gamble with their lives. There are people who are addicted to gambling just like there are people who are addicted to smoking. With gambling, people can lose their money, but with smoking, people can lose their lives. Every year over 400,000 people die from smoking related diseases. How many people die from gambling related problems? It is much better for people to bet with their money than to bet with their lives..

In a casino people pay to play games. The odds of winning vary from very high to very low. What most people do not understand is that those that gamble in a casino win. They do not win what they want to win, but they win. Gamblers call these winnings "small hits." These "small hits" are often much more than a gambler started with. If the gamblers left with the "small winning" they would always leave with more money than they came in with. But casinos count on the fact that gamblers will not be satisfied with "small winnings." They design the casinos to convince the gamblers that they have a chance to hit a big jackpot. The odds of hitting a big jackpot are very, very small. The odds of hitting a small jackpot are 50 to 100 percent. Because the "small jackpots" are not what the gamblers want they put it all back with the hope that they will hit a large jackpot

Playing slot machines is simply paying to play a game. In a casino it is called gambling. Paying to play games is a common activity in all areas of our lives. When we pay to play video games at a video arcade, it is no different than paying to play a slot machine. The play is the same except there is a chance to win the money back when a slot machine is played. Both have the thrill of winning and losing. We pay to play a wide variety of games at video arcades, county fairs, and amusement parks. The video arcade business is big business. It is worth nine billion dollars. It is worth more than the California movie business and more than all the casinos yearly take in Nevada.

Not only do we pay to play games we also pay to watch others play. Tickets for the playoff games between the Angels and the Yankees in the 2002 year series were selling for over $2,000. The average amount of money that is spent to watch a professional sports game far exceeds the average amount that is spent in a casino.

It is hypocritical to pay to play a game that you like but think that it is wrong for a person to pay to play a game that he or she likes simply because it is in a casino. It is hypocritical to criticize a person who gambles with his or her money in a casino but ignore a person who gambles with his or her life.

We live in a society where it is legal for children to play video arcade machine but illegal for children to play slot machines. When they play video arcade machines they have absolute no chance of getting their money back.. Which one is throwing money away? If gambling is taking a chance, then playing video arcade machines is not gambling because there is zero chance of getting the money back. As a result the video arcade business is making nine billion dollars while the casinos of Nevada are only making seven billion dollars

There is the thrill of winning when playing video arcade machines or slot machines. The video arcade machine gives only the thrill of winning. The slot machine gives not only the thrill of winning a game but also the thrill of winning money. People do not expect to get rich playing video arcade machines but they do expect to get rich with each spin of the slot machine. This unfulfilled expectation is what can cause depression and frustration. Those who play for fun, not expecting to get rich, get what they expect. The odds are against those who go to a casino expecting to get rich. Many lose all of their money chasing large jackpots. Nevertheless, gambling and losing money is small compared to the chance that people take when they gamble with their lives. Money lost when gambling can be replaced. Health lost when gambling is difficult to recover. Life lost when gambling is gone forever The biggest bet of all is the one where people bet on whether there is or is not a God. Gamblers call this type of bet an "all or nothing bet". Winners and losers will know the results at death. Good gamblers seldom bet against the odds.

Abstinence

Your mama was wrong about abstinence. One reason society has such a difficult time getting young people to practice abstinence is because young people are confused over what to abstain from. Does abstinence mean abstain from sexual intercourse or does it mean abstain from all sexual activity? There is no doubt about what sexual intercourse is. There is much confusion about what acts are considered sex. When does sex start? Can people be sexually active and not have sexual intercourse? What is it about sex that causes people to pursue it at the cost of jobs, reputations, and careers? Young people are taught to practice abstinence while all around them they see their parents, their politicians, their teachers and their preachers involved in sexual misconduct. A problem is caused because sex is overrated. Another problem is caused when people misunderstand the purpose of sexual intercourse. The main purpose of sexual intercourse is reproduction. The main purpose of sex is pleasure. This pleasure is caused by the presence of endorphins that are released by the brain during sexual activity. It is this " natural high " that comes from endorphins that causes men and women, boys and girls, young and old, married and single, to seek sex at almost any cost. At the moment of orgasm there is a 200% increase in the release of endorphins giving the individual the most pleasurable feeling that a human can have. Once young people become aware of the pleasure that comes from orgasm during partner sex, it becomes almost impossible to teach them to practice abstinence.

Sexual intercourse is a physical act that is the result of a choice. There are, however, many other sexual acts that are not a matter of choice. These sexual acts may be mental or emotional. These sexual acts also produce endorphins that are released by a visual or auditory stimuli. Not only do endorphins give pleasure but they are also believed to enhance the immune system, relieve pain, reduce stress and postpone aging. In other words endorphins are beneficial to health.

Sexual desire is a natural part of being human. Without sexual desire humans would not procreate. Since sexual desire is natural, young people should not feel guilty when they have such desire for the opposite sex. Sexual feelings come from God. Where as it is possible to practice abstinence from sexual intercourse, it is impossible to practice abstinence from sex. This is because sex can include everything from a thought to an orgasm. The teaching that people should practice abstinence assumes that sex is bad. Sex is good and natural. But like all things good it can be abused and misused

Abstinence from sexual intercourse is what society should teach. Sexual intercourse is the only sexual activity that can lead to parenthood. Only those who are ready and able to have and raise a child should have sexual intercourse. It is natural for people to express themselves through sexual activity. It is irresponsible for people to have sexual intercourse if they are not ready to assume the responsibility of parenthood. Even married couples can be irresponsible in the way they have sexual intercourse. They should not have more children than they can afford. Sexual intercourse is not an activity that is needed for good married sex. Good orgasms are needed for good sex. Sexual intercourse is just foreplay to orgasm-usually for men. Sexual intercourse is just one way to reach orgasm. For many men and women it is an inferior way to reach orgasm. Sexual intercourse is often a selfish masculine activity. Many women feel used after sexual intercourse. Although many women reach orgasm through sexual intercourse, most do not Because sexual intercourse is often a selfish masculine activity, it should be abstained from until a couple is ready to have children. It is responsible to abstain from sexual intercourse. It is humanly impossible to abstain from sexual activity. Humans are born with the ability to have orgasms. Many babies have orgasms in the first month of life. Abstaining from sex is impossible.. Humans are born sexual. William Masters reported that " Innumerable baby boys were born with fully erect organs. He also noted that all girl babies lubricated vaginally in the first four to six hours of life. Infants were born ready and fully equipped. During sleep, spontaneous erections or vaginal lubrications occur every eighty to ninety minutes throughout the entire life span." <u>Sex Without Shame</u> p.12 by Dr. Alayne Yates. It is irresponsible and ignorant to tell boys to practice abstinence. It would be unnatural because boys have "wet dreams" or nocturnal orgasms, which occur without encouragement or permission. A nocturnal orgasm is an involuntary sexual activity. In other words, abstaining from sexual intercourse is a choice. Abstaining from sex is not a choice.

The Virgin Myth

Your mama was wrong when she said men want to marry virgins. It is not true. It is a myth. It has been said that men want to have a lot of premarital sex, but when they get ready to marry they want to marry a virgin. Where did this idea come from? Nothing can be further from the truth. Most men don't marry virgins because the majority of women who marry are not virgins. The simple fact is that few women marry the first man that they have sex with. A lot of men say that they want to have sex with a virgin, but most could care less about marrying a virgin. Who has ever heard a man say, " I WANT TO MARRY A VIRGIN"? Women say it, but men do not even think about it. Women believe it and teach it, but it is not true. Men want a woman who has some sexual experience, but they do not want a woman who has " slept around."

One of the problems that may occur when a virgin marries is sexual frigidity. She may not know how to give or receive sexual pleasure. This can cause sexual dysfunction within the marriage. The myth says that a woman who is not a virgin will end up comparing her mate to her other sex partners, but on the contrary, a virgin may end up fantasizing about what it would be like having sex with someone else. Of course this also happens to men who are virgins when they marry. The virgin may also have the tendency to be inhibited. He or she may want to have sex in only one way- the way he or she first had sex. As a result, the experienced partner may seek for variety outside of the marriage. Everyone who marries should be sexually experienced. It is possible to be sexually active and experienced without having sexual intercourse. A person can abstain from sexual intercourse and still be sexually active. Having knowledge

31

and experience of how the sex organs of both the male and female work, is an important part of the growth process. Sexual intercourse, however, is different. It is a sex act that has the potential of uniting a couple permanently. With the birth of a child the two individuals will become united. They may divorce but they will always be united because of the child. It is for this reason that sexual intercourse should be limited to those who are ready to be parents. This applies only to young women because those who are past childbearing years are not valued for their virginity. In fact, Webster's New World Dictionary defines " virgin " as " a young woman who has not had sexual intercourse." After a woman passes the age of thirty, society becomes more concerned with her becoming a mother than remaining a virgin. Some women are choosing to become single mothers. Society also has two sets of moral laws- one for young women and one for older women. If a man and woman who are senior citizens take a trip alone, no one will question their morality, but if a young man and woman take a trip alone, their morality will be questioned. Many people in society can not imagine senior citizens being interested in sex. Because they believe that sex is for the young, they also believe that virginity is for the young. Of course they are wrong. Virginity is for anyone who wants to be a virgin. Most men are looking for love and they could care less if the woman is or is not a virgin.

There is nothing wrong with teaching a young woman to remain a virgin until marriage, but it is wrong to teach her to remain a virgin because men want to marry virgins. Virginity is something that concerns women, not men. Besides, sex with a virgin can be a very uncomfortable experience. Penetration can be difficult and painful. It often does not live up to its expectation. Most women do not have orgasms in their first sexual intercourse. In fact, some women never have an orgasm during sexual intercourse. In reality, sexual intercourse is an overrated form of "foreplay". It is foreplay to orgasm. Orgasm is the maximum level of sexual pleasure. Sexual intercourse is not needed in order to reach orgasm. People can have a very active sex life without having sexual intercourse. It is a myth that intercourse is "going all the way". Orgasm is "going all the way". If men can reach orgasm without sexual intercourse, they will do so. Women who know this will never be pressured to have sexual intercourse. Because some men are so interested in receiving and not giving oral sex, transvestites can fool them. It has become popular today for young women to perform oral sex on young men. The young women should not do so unless the young men return the favor. Rather than return the favor many young men will simply stop asking. Sexual pleasure should always be mutual. If it is not then someone is being used.

If a young woman wants to remain a virgin she can do so and still be sexually active. Sexual intercourse should be reserved for the individual who wants children or the individual who is ready for parenthood.. Sexual intercourse is not needed in order to reach maximum pleasure in orgasm. After all, what both individuals want is orgasm-with or without intercourse.

The "Virgin Myth" says that as long as a woman has not had sexual intercourse she is a virgin. This view completely ignores the woman who gives and receives oral sex. It also ignores the woman who has anal sex. Is a woman still a virgin if she performs mutual masturbation? Who is or is not a virgin depends on the definition used. Because all humans are sexually active almost from the moment of birth, it is impossible for anyone to be a virgin.

Good Porno?

Your mama was wrong about pornography. If it is wrong to watch others have sex, then sex itself must be wrong. The first time that humans had sex, God was watching. If a film had been made would that film be pornographic? Our society is so backward that we call the most pleasurable activity known to man nasty, vulgar, dirty, bad and pornographic. The union of humans in sex for the purpose of reproduction and pleasure is part of nature. Without sex the human race would die out. The problem with pornography is not the sex, it is the abusive way that sex is portrayed. The sex act is one of the most enjoyable experiences known to humans. It is also nature's way of continuing the species. Not only does our society abuse sex it also uses abusive language to describe sex. Many of our obscene and vulgar words are used to describe things related to sex. There is, however, nothing obscene or vulgar about sex or the sex organs. Sex and the things related to sex are good but can be used in a bad way. Sex is natural. It is nature's way of reproducing. Society should be just as comfortable talking about the sex organs as it is talking about the other body parts. Our society calls the genitals " private parts " One meaning of the word " private " is " not open to the public." It would seem that since the genitals are special, being the source of life, they would be publicly celebrated. In fact, in many past cultures the sex act was part of religious ceremony.

Pornography is a word that is associated with anything sexual. It usually means sex acts that are seen by others. It may be live, on film, in books or in still pictures. Some call nudity pornography. Unfortunately those who consider pornography bad are often the same ones who think that sex is bad. In the Judeo-Christian culture the first thing that God told man to do was have sex. Before man was told what his job or diet was to be, he was told to have sex. To God it was so important that He told them three times: Be fruitful, multiply, and replenish the earth. God said that everything that He had made was good. Having sex for reproduction and pleasure was part of God's original plan for humans. Babies are born fully capable of having orgasms. Many have orgasms within the first month of life. Boy babies are often born with fully erect penises. It is hard to believe that God turned His head in shame when Adam and Eve had sex for the first time. It is more reasonable to assume that God was the First Sex Educator. Sex was not something to be shamefully done in secret.

What is wrong with pornography is not the fact that it depicts others having sex but that it depicts others having abusive sex. People are shown a warped and twisted way of having sex. Warped and twisted sex is wrong. Something is wrong if it is forced, harmful or dangerous to others. Some are uncomfortable watching others have sex. They believe that if something is uncomfortable it must be wrong. History has shown that using comfort for determining what is right or wrong has been dangerous for many. Discrimination against blacks in America was legal for years because many whites were uncomfortable with the idea of associating with blacks. Discrimination was legal but it was wrong because it was forced and harmful to others. If something is not forced, harmful or dangerous and contributes to the enjoyment of life, then it is good. Just because people feel shame or discomfort about something, does not mean it is wrong. If people feel shame when doing things that are natural there is something lacking in their education. Shame is not natural- it is learned.

Although pornography in general is wrong because of the warped depiction of sex, there are some good things about it. By watching pornography some people learn for the first time what the sex organs of the opposite sex look like. It is hard to believe but true that there are some married women with children who have never seen an erect penis! Therefore, they have sex in the dark with their clothes on. They have been taught to believe that sex is dirty and nasty. On a recent talk show, a married lady with two girls said that the penis was the ugliest thing that God created. There are also individuals who when young would often have sex while their friends watched and while they watched their friends. These youthful activities

35

were considered bad and a way of rebelling against parents. In adulthood these same activities which were enjoyed as youths became secretive and shameful. Such is not the case in all cultures nor has it been the case in cultures of the past

In the South Pacific Island of Mangia, privacy is unheard of. Families often live in a one-room hut with five to sixteen members of all ages (not unlike the one- room log cabins in early America). It is common for young girls to entertain lovers at night and for young children to hear the sound of their parent's moist genitals as they make love. Young girls also learn from elderly women who teach by telling stories and by direct practical instruction. Sex Without Shame, p.71 by Dr. Alayne Yates.

In most early cultures, the birth of a baby was a family event in which all participated. Children helped deliver their new brothers and sisters. It was not shameful to see the mother's vagina as the baby came out. Even today, children are sometimes called upon in an emergency to help deliver their new baby brother or sister. Society calls them brave little heroes.

Why is it that society will not tolerate parents who have sex in front of their children but will tolerate verbal and physical abuse for years? This is not to advocate parents having sex while their children watch but is to question why one is considered more harmful than the other. Even women, who are the victims of verbal and physical abuse, think that having sex while children watch is far more harmful. Surely watching people being abusive to each other can not be less harmful than watching people making love to each other. Yet, our society by its values and laws teach that watching violence is less harmful than watching sex.

There is a big need for people to see sex in a loving and caring atmosphere. Seeing this kind of sex should in no way be classified as pornographic. It would simply be watching humans do a very natural and beautiful act. Society would like to ignore the fact that God watched the very first humans have sex. There is a great need for society to depict sex in a loving and caring relationship. The sex act is beautiful, but the adult film industry often portrays it in an abusive and ugly way.

The definition of pornography according to Webster's New World Dictionary is "writings or pictures intended primarily to arouse sexually." One problem with this is that what might be sexually arousing to one person may not be sexually arousing to another. Another problem is that it assumes that being sexually aroused is bad. As said in the beginning, sex is natural and good. Sex is bad when it is forced, abusive and selfish. In other words, writings and pictures about sex are neither good nor bad, it all depends on whether the sex depicted is good or bad. Therefore, pornography (writings or pictures which sexually arouse) can be good or bad.

Homosexuality

Your mama was wrong about homosexuality. It will come as a big surprise to many in society to know that humans come in more than two sexes. Males and females are just opposite ends of a continuum that includes a variety of sexual forms. If a homosexual is a person who is attracted to someone of the same sex, what is a person who is neither male nor female? There are males and there are females and there are intersex people. Intersex people are those who are born with varying characteristics of both sexes. According to a Web site by Emily Nussbuam, intersexuality occurs in about one of every 2,000 births. Nine types of intersexuality have been identified in humans. Any intelligent discussion of homosexuality must include an understanding of intersexuality. In the following material the nine types of intersex conditions are defined: (1) Gonadal intersex (true hermaphrodite) in which the child has both male and female genitals, (2). Congenital adrenal hyperplasia in which the genitals of female children are masculinized to a degree, (3). Androgen insensitivity syndrome (AIS) where a child has the XY male chromosomes and the external anatomy and identity of the female but lacks the reproductive organs of either (4). Partial AIS where the child may exhibit some male secondary sex characteristics if the testes are not removed. (5).Hypospadias where the urethral meatus (opening) is on the underside or base of the penis. This is not necessarily an intersexed condition just abnormal. (6). Mayer-Rokitansky-Kustur-Hauser syndrome has all of the visible signs of a female but no vagina, cervix, uterus, or fallopian tubes. These individuals are genetically males, (XY chromosomes). They may develop breasts but fail to menstruate. From childhood they feel and think like a male. (7). Vaginal agenesis where the vagina does not form and there is the MRKH syndrome. (8).

Cloacal exstrophy (a condition in which there is malformation of the pelvis and no penis.) They develop a male identity even if surgically made a female. (9). Klinefelter's syndrome (Genetic males with XXY or XXXY chromosomes) Turner's syndrome are individuals who are anatomically female but have one X and no Y chromosome. They are short in stature and fail to develop secondary sex characteristics. These nine forms have been listed because they should be known if an individual wishes to speak intelligently about homosexuality. How can society call an individual a homosexual if society does not know what sex the individual is?

Most intersex people grow up confused and ashamed because of an accident of birth. Our society protects and cares for other people with disabilities and abnormalities but intersex people are ridiculed and condemned. They find it difficult and painful to live in a world where the majority of people are either male or female. They often face religious and social discrimination, not because of what they choose to be but because of how they were born. Some obese religious leaders who call homosexuality a sin fail to see their own sin of overeating. They are hypocrites and lack understanding.

It has only been in the last few years that society has begun to understand the plight of these people. However, prejudice and hatred still runs rampant. This is because most of the negative attitudes toward homosexuals are based upon a misunderstanding of the purpose of sex. Our society does not talk about sex except in a degrading or comical way. Sexual activity is not discussed in an open and natural way. Many grow up thinking that sex itself is dirty. Society does not openly talk about the sex organs and it certainly does not talk about people who have both sex organs. Intersex people live among us but few of us know who they are. They do not tell and we do not ask. In a report by Dr. Ann Fausto-Sterling of Brown University, it was estimated that one in 100 are born with bodies that differ from the standard male or female. She also reported that one or two in 1,000 babies receive surgery to 'normalize' genital appearance. (Intersex Society of North America Web Site.) Before individuals call someone else "gay, homo, or faggot," it might be wise to find out if the individual was born with sexual organs that are anatomically different. How do people know if someone is a homosexual if they do not know the sex of the person? Just because a person has a penis does not mean the person is a male. The person could be male on the outside and female on the inside. In fact, all humans start out as female. The scar that all males have that runs from the anus to the tip of the penis is the closed up opening where the vagina would have been. When the male hormone from the testes works properly, it turns the fetus into a male. Few males know why they are born with this permanent scar.

The " F " Word

Your mama was wrong about dirty words. Words are not dirty or vulgar. They have meaning only in the context in which they are used. Words are just sounds used to express thoughts and feelings. A word in one time and place may have another meaning in another time and place. A word may mean one thing to a young person and something completely different to an older person. Words that only a few years ago were considered offensive and improper are today considered proper and acceptable. For example, many women no longer consider the word "girl" a compliment. To them it is offensive and demeaning. The word "nigger" has a different meaning when used by a black man among blacks than when used by a white man among blacks. In other words the meaning of a word is often dependent upon the context. Another example is the word "gay". Years ago if people said that a party was "gay" it had a different meaning than it does today. So it is with many curse words. People are offended by the words "shit" and "fuck". However, these words did not start out as offensive but as a common way for Anglo-Saxons to express themselves.

The English speaking Anglo-Saxons were considered inferior by the French speaking Normans. In 1066 The French speaking Normans conquered the Anglo-Saxons and became the ruling caste. When the two languages became blended together into Middle English, the ruling Normans rejected many of the Anglo-Saxons words calling them crude and offensive. In 1380 the universities of Oxford and Cambridge adopted English as the official language. Both Norman words and Saxon words were included but many of the Saxon's words were considered improper. The words were considered improper not because they were offensive but because they were used by the Saxons. The Norman word "perspiration" was proper while the

Anglo-Saxon word "sweat" was improper. The Norman word "urine" was proper but the Saxon word "piss" was improper. The Norman word "excrement" was proper while the Saxon word "shit" was improper. So it was with one of society's most offensive words "fuck". It was considered improper but the Norman word "fornicate" was accepted as respectable. Originally the Old English word "fokken" was a word with the meaning "to beat against". In our society "fuck" is a vulgar word used to describe sexual intercourse. It is also used by some to express anger. Just a few years ago the word "pregnant" was considered improper for polite company. The words "ass" and "butt" were censored from the airwaves. Now they are accepted. Many of the music lyrics heard in today's songs would not have been recorded years ago. Today these songs sell for millions of dollars. If history is any predictor of the future, the words "shit" and "fuck" will become acceptable in a few years. Until then it is wise for people to refrain from using offensive words unless they are prepared to accept the consequences.

Many of these curse words are called adult words. But young people use these words a lot more than adults. Adults who are educated and polite use these words in a limited way. Many school children use obscene words in their everyday language. Vulgar and offensive words that are seldom heard on a college campus are commonly heard on Middle and High school campuses. They seem to be used not only as a way of communication, but also as a way for those with low self-esteem to get attention. It is as if the young people want to say "Look at me! I am old enough to say what I want!" The only problem is that they think that cursing is a way to show maturity. However, in reality, it is a sign of immaturity and limited language development. Immaturity is shown when people use words that are knowingly offensive to others. Mature people are sensitive to the feelings of others. Mature people know the difference between knowing what is right to say and having the right to say it. In other words, it is not always right to say what you have a right to say. The mature considers the feelings of others.

Religion is Hearsay

Your mama was wrong about God. People believe that their religious views are right and true. People shape their lives by the standards and values of their religious beliefs. Many religious beliefs have a history that is thousands of years old. However, regardless of what the religious belief is, it is still hearsay. Even if it is true, it is still hearsay. It is hearsay if it was not personally witnessed. Hearsay by definition is hearing what someone else said happened. Most religions started hundreds or thousands of years ago. They are accounts by individuals of events that they said happened. These events may in fact, have happened, but they will always be what someone else said happened. In is interesting to note that when someone reads from a religious book, he or she is reading an account of what someone said happened. IT IS HEARSAY. The majority .of the major religions were founded by men who said that God gave them a message. Most of the religions see women as inferior to men. Many individuals will quote from their religious writings as if they are quoting the very words of God. The truth of the matter is that they are only quoting what someone said that God said. Their belief is not in what God said but in what someone said that God said. In the Bible, God is said to have told Eve, "thy desire shall be to thy husband, and he shall rule over thee."' (Genesis 3:16) .God may have said the words but they were still written by a man who said, " God said". Because many individuals fail to recognize this important fact, they become convinced that they are following the very words of God A lot of pain and suffering has been caused by those who believed that they were doing the will of God.

These religions have been passed down from generation to generation. For years they have been accepted as the truth. Any disagreement with these long held beliefs will end in controversy and conflict. Who can say how many wars have been fought because of a religious disagreement? The continuing conflict in the Middle East is basically about religion. Many think that a belief must be true if it has been believed in for hundreds or thousands of years. But believing something is true will not make it true no matter how many people believe it or how many years it has been believed. At one time people believed that the world was flat, but their belief did not make it flat. Truth is independent of what one believes. Truth never changes, but what people believe is true, does change.. People believed that man would never fly, but when flying became a reality, their long held beliefs became obsolete. Many religious leaders said that it was not God's will for man to go to the moon. When man went to the moon it became obvious that these religious leaders did not know the will of God.

Some religious people are so convinced that they are right that they will refuse to accept any facts that do not agree with their beliefs. Even when facts and reality clearly show them to be wrong, they will not change. They would rather appear right than be right. This refusal to change explains why many reformers of the past have been rejected and killed. History has shown that the majority of people are often wrong.

"What is right is seldom popular and what is popular is seldom right". One writer puts it this way, " The highway to hell is broad and its gate is wide enough for the multitudes who choose its easy way. But the Gateway to life is small and the road is narrow, and only a few ever find it." (Matthew 7:13) The poet Robert Frost called it "The Road Less Traveled." The search for truth will always continue as long as people recognize that most of what they believe is true is really just hearsay. It becomes a fact only when it is observed, tested, and finally predictions made from those observations.

When individuals get on an airplane they must believe that it will not crash or they will not get on it. They cannot say for a fact that it will not crash, they can only have faith that it will not crash. This faith is based upon past observations and experiences. The faith becomes a fact of reality when the plane lands safely. The reality of the safe landing does away with the faith or belief that the plane will land safely. Faith or belief is no longer needed when face to face with reality. Faith and religious beliefs are often shrouded in the darkness of ignorance. Reality is the light that dispels the darkness that may exist in long held religious beliefs. As darkness cannot co-exist with light, neither can myths co-exist with reality.

A religion is a belief. A belief is an idea that has not been proven. When it is proven to be true or a fact, it no longer is a belief. This is true not only of religion but also of history and science. If it cannot be tested and observed, then it must remain in the realm of belief. A religious or historical event may be true, but it is hearsay if it is based upon what someone else said happened. This reality covers almost everything that is encountered. Whatever people believe they must never forget that if it was not personally experienced, it is hearsay.

There are many people who are willing to die for what they believe even though these beliefs are hearsay. However, it is very wrong to be willing to kill someone for a belief that is only hearsay. Dying for one's religion may be honorable, but what can justify killing in the name of religion?

Religious myths affect society in many ways. Views about right and wrong are often based upon religious traditions. For example, a woman will go to a strange man and let him examine her breasts and genitals because he is a medical doctor. But this same woman will think that it is immoral and wrong for a man who is a friend or relative to see her naked. Why does society assume that only medical doctors know how to act properly around a naked woman? Does society think that a man automatically receives a clean mind when he receives his medical degree? Long held religious traditions say one is right and the other is wrong. Common sense says that society is wrong. Here again people are judging what is right or wrong by how uncomfortable they feel.

Many religious people see their spiritual leaders as more than human. They become upset at the thought of a "Holy Man" sitting on the stool and having a bowel movement. However, no matter how "holy" he is, he still has to take care of the call of nature.

Marrying Relatives

Your mama wrong about relatives marrying each other. Society says that individuals who marry close relatives are committing incest. Webster's New World Dictionary defines incest as, " Sexual intercourse between persons too closely related to marry legally" In other words, it is only incest if it is illegal. In the United States of America, most people are ignorant of the laws that relate to close relatives marrying. If people are asked if their state follows the "biblical" or "western" model in the laws about marriage, they will look at you with a blank stare. Basically the "biblical" model bans in-laws from marrying but permits cousins, while the "western" model bans cousins from marrying but permits in-laws. There are seven states that have laws that follow the "biblical" model, twenty-two states that have laws that follow the "western" model, six states that combine characteristics of both and nine states that follow neither. This means that a marriage may be legal in one state but illegal in another. Some people base their idea of what is right and wrong upon how it makes them feel. If they feel uncomfortable, they say it is wrong. If they feel comfortable, they say it is right. Many would rather be comfortable and wrong than uncomfortable and right. They would rather appear right than be right.

People have been marrying close relatives from the beginning of recorded history. How could the world have become populated if people had not married relatives? Are we not all descendants from the same parents? The three major religions all claim Abraham as their ancestor-Islam, Judaism, and Christianity. Abraham was married to his sister. He said in Genesis 20:12, "And yet indeed she is my sister; she is the daughter of my father, but not the daughter of my mother." Most people who read this dismiss it by saying, "It was O.K. then." By saying so they admit that morality is relative to the time and culture. What was considered right in one time and place may be considered wrong in another time and place. When Abraham, who was married to his sister, decided it was time for Isaac to marry, he chose a bride from among his own family. Jacob married two sisters who were also his first cousins Moses instructed the daughters of Zelophehad to marry only "the family of the tribe of their father." Numbers 36:6.

What is a race or tribe of people except descendants that consistently married among themselves? They have reproduced traits that distinguish them from other races or tribes. This is why there are different races. There are Japanese people because the Japanese people married among themselves. They married within their "family". The same is true of all the other races.

Most people in our society are very uncomfortable with the idea of a brother and sister marrying. However, there is no indication that the people in Abraham's day had any problem with him marrying Sarah, his sister. Today, Abraham would be called a sexual pervert. He certainly could not belong to any traditional church. The only reason our society thinks it is wrong for a brother and sister to marry is because it is not part of our customs. It is hard to conceive of a time in the near future when a marriage between a brother and a sister will be accepted. Although there are some in society who have married their sibling, most people can not imagine doing such a thing-even if Abraham did.

There should be no laws or regulations prohibiting mature adults from choosing how they want to live their lives. Society may not like the way individuals choose to live and may be uncomfortable with their lifestyles, nevertheless every adult is endowed by his or her creator with certain "unalienable rights" such as "life, liberty, and the pursuit of happiness." No person, religion, or government has the right to force a person to go against his or her will. As long as a person's rights do not interfere with the rights of another, he or she should be left alone. There should however, be some regulation that will prohibit older siblings from taking advantage of younger siblings. This means that there should be a law preventing older siblings from marrying siblings who are five or more years younger. This is not by any means advocating marriage between close relatives, rather it is simply saying that marriage between close relatives has a history that goes back thousands of years.

People who are uncomfortable with siblings marrying will seek to pass laws that control what others do. This causes conflict. The source of most human conflict can be traced to the desire to control the lives of others. It does not matter whether the conflict is between husbands and wives or between one nation and another. Many people are uncomfortable if they are not in control of others. Peace, however, does not come from having control of others but from having self-control.

Teacher Certification

Your mama was wrong about teacher certification. There are a lot of people who are teaching who should not be and a lot of people who should be teaching but are not. They are not teaching because the states say that they are not qualified. In order to be qualified to teach in many states, individuals must be college graduates or pass some kind of test. However, graduating from college and passing a test does not qualify people to teach. Teachers must have something to teach and be able to teach it. The ability to teach can be obtained inside or outside of college. Many states have an elitist attitude when it comes to certifying people to teach. This attitude deprives young people of some of the most talented people available. Something is wrong with a society when the founder of Microsoft, a computer company, is not qualified to teach computer science. He is not qualified because he is not a college graduate. Something is wrong with a society when a major music star is not qualified to teach music in its schools. Something is wrong with a society when an Olympic gold medal swimmer is not qualified to teach swimming in its schools.

There is concern that there is a major shortage of qualified teachers. The problem is not a shortage of qualified people. The problem is the way people are certified to teach. Every year colleges and universities bestow honorary degrees on individuals who have distinguished themselves in certain specific fields. After many years of experience they have become experts in their fields. The same thing could be done in education. States could give honorary teaching credentials to individuals who have become experts in their fields. People who have been composing and performing music for a living would be much more qualified to teach music than a recent college graduate would be with a BA degree in music. States however, will not certify them because they are not college graduates. As a result students miss out on the opportunity to be educated by some of the world's most talented people.

Those who are certified to teach should be paid according to their knowledge and experience. This should apply whether they are State certified teachers, honorary certified teachers, or substitute teachers. If a business expects to succeed, will it pay the same amount to people with one year of experience that it pays to people with thirty years of experience? This practice is one of the major weaknesses of the educational system. It is harmful and has outlived its usefulness.

Parents Owe Children

Your mama was wrong when she said that children owe their parents. To owe means to be obligated to pay back. Why should a person be obligated to pay a debt that was forced upon him or her? How can a person be born into debt? The parents owe the child because the parents made a choice to bring a baby that needed to be protected and cared for into the world. The parents chose to take on the obligation of protecting and caring for the child. This obligation stops only when the child becomes able to be a parent. The grown child can choose to be are not to be a parent.

If children choose to become parents, they become obligated to protect and care for their children. At no time are children indebted to their parents. They owe their parents nothing. The parents chose to be financially responsible for their children. In other words, they took on the debt of raising children. Being born is not a choice, being a parent is. It is the duty of parents to protect and care for children until the children can protect and care for themselves. Humans are the only beings that expect their offspring's to thank them for taking care of them. Children thank their parents by becoming independent adults. The debt that parents owe their children is paid in full when the children no longer need their parents. Grown, independent children, free their parents. If for some reason the children do not become independent enough to be able to protect and to care for themselves, the parents must do so. In general, the parent's responsibility ends when the children reach adulthood. All the problems that children face in the world are the result of being born-NO BIRTH, NO PROBLEMS.

In many past cultures, parents felt that it was their duty to leave an inheritance to their children. They believed that even after death they had a continuing responsibility to their children. In modern society this view has been reversed. Today it is believed that children are responsible for their parent's welfare. This view has contributed to the increased amount of poverty among senior citizens. Parents should work hard in their youth and accumulate an inheritance for their children. Most, unfortunately, fail to save and end up squandering their means in an attempt to impress others. Often they end up in poverty with their children taking care of them. When this happens, the children are unable to save so that they can leave an inheritance for their own children. This should not be! Those who are here first should leave a smooth path for others to follow.

Study the cultures of the past. They accumulated knowledge and wealth and passed it on to the next generation. Progress of an individual or a nation is dependent upon the ability to use the knowledge and wealth of the previous generation. Those individuals and nations that fail to do this can not succeed. They are doomed to the past. They are constantly re-inventing the wheel. Many countries are still living like they did hundreds of years ago. Progress comes when people are determined to make life better for future generations. Nothing is perfect. There is a better way to do anything. Everything can be improved. Parents should expect their children to be better parents then they were. Parents should acknowledge their own mistakes in the hope that their children will not repeat them. Unfortunately, many children grow up emulating their parents, thus insuring the continuation of past imperfections. Children should challenge the values and traditions of their parents. They should seek to improve up on them. Each generation should make the world a better place for the next.

Lives of great men all remind us

We can make our lives sublime,

And, departing, leave behind us

Footprints on the sands of time.

Longfellow

It is not necessary to answer the question, "How can parents be successful?" Many books have been written on the subject. The question to be answered is "When do parents become successful?" Parents are successful when children no longer need protection or care. It is a basic law of nature that every creature must learn to protect and care for itself. The slowest and weakest become food for the fastest and strongest. It's "The survival of the fittest". The same can be said about humans. Those who survive develop the skills and knowledge that are needed, those who do not, fall through the cracks. They become failures. They sink to the level of permanent dependency on parents or institutions.

Individuals are mature when they reach the level where they can handle all of the ups and downs that they will face in life. It is sad to say that some never do. Those who never learn how to handle life will find even success destructive. They are unable to recognize the opportunities that come their way. The good parents teach their children not only how to live but also how to enjoy living.

Women's Lib

Your mama was wrong when she said that women want to be treated equally. The idea that women want to be treated as equal to men is a widely held myth. Few women want to be treated like men. In fact, many women believe that men are just overgrown, emotionally immature boys, who think about sex most of the time. If women were to be treated equally, they would no longer feel special because they would lose the many polite things that men now do. Women don't want to be treated equally they want to be treated fairly. They want equal pay for equal work. They want an equal opportunity to reach their full potential. They want society to understand that being different does not mean being inferior. Almost all societies have made distinctions between men and women. Female modesty has separated men from women. This modesty, however, is not defined the same in every culture, time, and place. In fact, history has shown that the definition of modesty changes within a culture in the course of time. What was immodest and unacceptable at one time often becomes modest and acceptable in another time. It is impossible to treat men and women as equals as long as female modesty exist. Female modesty declares that men and women are separate and different human beings. Cultures establish political and religious laws in order to support this view. Boys and girls are raised to believe that because women, in general, are smaller and weaker than men that they must also be inferior. Boys and girls must learn how men and women are expected to act in their culture. This culture may be as limited as a neighborhood or as broad as a nation. In other words, they learn what it means to be a man or a woman from those around them. They assume that the way people act is the way people should act. In many societies of the world women are seen as individuals who need to be protected and cared for by men. Individuals who are seen as unable to protect and care for themselves are considered inferior. As long as women need to be protected and cared for, they will be seen as inferior. There can be no equality in a society that has one set of laws for men and another for women. The separation will create discrimination. If a society wants to treat women as equals it must eliminate female modesty. There can not be laws that are legal for some and illegal for others. In many societies there are laws that make it illegal for a woman to go topless in public. These laws support female modesty. Because of female modesty, girls as young as three are required to cover up. Since they have no breasts to cover, the tops are just symbolic. Men who have large breasts because they are overweight or because they have well developed pectoral muscles are not required to wear tops. Modesty dictates that the nipples of females be covered. Society has come to accept tops that reveal all of the breasts but the nipples. If a transvestite, who has developed breasts because of hormonal treatment, goes topless in public, he will be arrested even though he is a man. However, he will not be placed in the women's section of the jail. Why is it legal for a man to go topless in public? The law also requires males to register for selective service when they reach eighteen. There is no such law for females. The law should treat all citizens as equals. Equal rights should include equal responsibility. If the law looks upon women as humans who need men to protect and care for them, then the law looks upon women as unequal

Our society has many customs that support the idea of women being inferior. Men are taught to open doors for women, to pull out chairs for women, to let women go first, to carry heavy things for women, and to pick up things that women drop. Men are not expected to do such things for other men. All of these things support the view that women are special and therefore should be treated in a special way. How is it possible to be special and equal at the same time? No matter how liberated women may think they are, they still want to feel special. They still expect their husbands to get up and check on a strange noise that may be heard at night. They revert to the position of unequal humans that needs to be protected. If women think they are equal to men, they will have no problem working while the men stay at home. After all, that is what men have been doing for years.. Many liberated women still feel uncomfortable about telling how old they are or their weight. Men have no such feelings. When women make such minor things important, they reinforce the idea that they are special. They don't want to be treated like men, they want to be treated special. They want female modesty to always remain.

Some women spend a large amount of time and energy focusing on how they look. It is a characteristic of the young and immature to judge people by their outward appearance. People should not be judged by their sex or skin color. As people mature they learn that there is more to individuals than outward appearance. This obsession of many women to look forever young and beautiful is a product of female modesty. It teaches that women should act and look totally different from men in order to be attractive. Women are expected to look a certain way, dress a certain way, talk a certain way, and walk a certain way. Men are expected to do the opposite. The result is inequality. How can it be otherwise? These separate roles for men and women are even seen in the way they relate to each other sexually. Men are to be aggressive and women are to be passive. Discomfort is often the case when these roles are reversed. It is proper and good to want to dress and look fit and trim. But to think that one's dress and outward appearance determines one's worth can cause problems.

The military has been affected by female modesty. In an attempt to treat women as equals, the courts have forced the military to accept women in institutions that have been traditionally all men. The women are not accepted as equals but as women. In order to do this, the institutions have had to make changes to accommodate female modesty. If women are to be truly accepted as equals in the military, female modesty must be eliminated. Women must train with men, eat with men, exercise with men, shower with men, and sleep in the same barracks with men. This will mean that both men and women will learn the true meaning of self-control. The military prides itself in teaching self- control and self- discipline. The ability to control sexual desire will be a true test. Control of sexual desire is the ultimate in self-discipline. It is the one area that many of our political and religious leaders have failed to master.

There will always be sexual assaults and sexual harassment in a society that maintains female modesty. Female modesty draws attention to the differences between males and females. Female clothes often are designed to emphasize the sexual differences between males and females. Males are more attracted to a clothed female than a nude female. This is very obvious in a nude strip club where the men lose interest in the female as soon as she becomes nude. One hour later when she comes out with clothes on, the men become interested again. This loss of interest is even more obvious when both sexes are nude. Nudity equalizes the sexes. In an unpublished paper in 1939, Abraham Maslow wrote " I have the feeling that a spread of nudism would be a step in the direction of greater ease and equality for men and women,." The Right to be Human p.135. As was written earlier, modesty supports inequality. Men and women will never be truly liberated until female modesty is eliminated..

As long as society continues to use modesty in order to separate the sexes, there will be inequality. Society does not want to ignore the differences between the sexes. It uses female modesty to draw attention to these differences. Female modesty is a very important part of totalitarian government. When a dictator comes to power one of the first things he does is establish a dress code for women. The same is often true of many religions. Female modesty supports the idea that men are superior to women.

Overweight

Your mama was wrong about being fat. Society says that a person should not stop loving another just because he or she gains weight. Love has nothing to do with being fat or thin. If a person gains weight or deliberately changes his or her physical appearance so that he or she is no longer considered attractive, it would be a fact of great denial to expect one's mate to change what he or she finds attractive. A mate may be deeply in love with the person but not in love with the fat. Because a mate is still in love with you, does not mean that he or she is still attracted to you. Everyone should do whatever he or she can do to stay as physically and sexually attractive on the outside as on the inside. If one does not, he or she may find his or her mate still in love but physically and sexually attracted to someone else. True love is unconditional. However, society should teach people the difference between loving the person and loving the fat. Some people think that fat is beautiful and attractive. However, no one can claim that fat is healthy. Individuals who are overweight face many health problems. Being overweight can also shorten individual's lives. Society places too much emphasis on losing weight in order to look good and not enough emphasis on losing weight for the sake of good health. Many people who are fat or overweight often say that they are happy and enjoy being fat. After losing weight these same people confess that they were lying about how they really felt. They say that they were very miserable and uncomfortable. Some say that they hated being fat. Since it is awkward and uncomfortable for a thin person to wipe his or her bottom after a bowel movement, it must be difficult or impossible for an obese person.

Since being overweight is so dangerous and unhealthy it would seem to be an act of love to encourage and help a loved one to lose weight. Many people have no problem telling their love ones that smoking is bad and can shorten their lives. These same people however, considered it impolite to tell a fat person that being overweight is unhealthy and can kill. Why is it right to sit by silently and watch the one that you love slowly commit suicide? Loving a disable person is not the same as loving the disability. Loving a blind person is not the same as loving the blindness. Likewise you can love the fat person without loving the fat.

How can an individual go about losing weight? What is the most effective way to lose weight? If an individual is serious about losing weight he or she must take the necessary steps. First, it must be understood that fat is unused energy. Fat comes in the calories that are eaten. The only way calories enter the body is through the mouth. In other words, people get fat from overeating, not from lack of exercise. Whenever people stop eating they lose weight. It is a matter of cause and effect. It is impossible to stay fat or gain weight without eating. Many of those who want to lose weight deny this fact. To lose weight, don't eat! Second, it must be understood that exercise contributes more to being fit than being trim. Being slim and trim is not the same as being fit. Just because a person is thin doesn't mean he or she is fit or healthy.

It is impossible to be overweight and healthy. Being overweight is bad for one's health. It is a permanent state of poor health. Some believe that obesity is more harmful than smoking. There are probably more people over 80 who smoke than people over 80 who are obese.

Why is it that people who are lost on the ocean or in the wilderness never gain weight? Can it be that they didn't have any food to eat? There has never been a case of an individual gaining weight while lost. It is an indisputable fact that people who are lost without food to eat will lose weight. Society can talk about fat cells, metabolism or thyroid problems, but if people are lost where they can not get anything to eat, they will lose weight-no ifs, ands, or butts.

Losing weight involves more than just eating less and exercising more. It involves eating and exercising in ways that contribute to good health. Eating less and exercising more will cause weight lost but not good health. Eating and exercising right will bring about weight loss and good health. Exercising will make you fit. Overeating will make you fat.

Date Rape

Your mama was wrong about date rape. The view that your mama has about sex creates an atmosphere where date rape can occur. Date rape can be prevented if society is willing to make some fundamental changes in its values and its ways of viewing sex. Society must understand how and why rape occurs. Sex in our society is viewed as something that is done in secret. This view must be changed. Some people call it "silent sex". People, in general, don't want others to know when they are having sex. Parents had "silent sex" because they didn't want to "wake up the kids". Children learned by example that sex was to be silent and secretive. This is one of the major changes that society needs to make. Sex should be private but not secret. "Silent sex" should be eliminated. There are many things that society does in private such as using the restroom, getting dress, and taking a shower. People may hear others using the restroom or taking a shower but they do not see them. It is done in private but not in secret. People grow up believing that sex should not be seen or heard. This view that sex should be done in complete secrecy prepares the stage not only for rape but also for date rape. People often go through great lengths to make sure that their sexual activity is done in isolation and secrecy.

Rape generally occurs in isolation and secrecy where there are no witnesses. This is also true of date rape. The date may not even have sex in mind until he finds himself alone with his mate. It is then that he realizes that forced sex is possible without any witnesses. Therefore, to avoid date rape it is absolutely imperative to never be alone with your date. In private, yes, in secret, never. Private means to be someplace where you could be heard but not seen. When a date ask you to go someplace where you can be alone to talk, tell him that you don't have to be alone to talk. You can talk anywhere. In a private room you can hug, kiss, and even have sex, if you want. But if there is someone in another room, and you are being forced to have sex, there is help just

60

a room away. The rapist does not want anyone to know what he is doing. Like Mom and Dad and society in general, the rapist believes that sex should be done in silence and in secret.

The first step in avoiding date rape is to stop viewing sex as something to be done secretly and silently. There is absolutely nothing wrong if people hear you having sex. Group dating should become a common activity. If couples were to date with other couples, they would provide some protection against rape. Group dating eliminates isolation and secrecy. Many past cultures considered sex as an open and sacred ceremony. There was no attempt to conceal or isolate. Rape is often said to be an act of control. Control over someone is easier in an isolated setting than in a setting where help is nearby.

Many men believe that it is their right to control women. Women are viewed as individuals who are inferior and who are in need of care and control. This is a wide spread view. It is particularly obvious during times of war and crisis. Society talks about protecting the women and children. Women are placed in the same category as children. In war, men are expected to take care of themselves, but women and children look to men for care and protection. As children obey the adults who take care of them so women are expected to obey the men who take care of them. Rape is a way for some men to say, " I am in control of you." Many husbands view their wives as inferior and in need of control. They sometimes rape their wives. It is rape if it is against an individual's will. When a woman is forced to have sex against her will, it is rape. Wife rape is probably the most common form of rape. It is difficult to prove because husbands and wives have sex in secret. Once again the view that sex should be done in secrecy creates the opportunity for rape to occur.

Women and children are often seen as the symbols of the future of a country. During war times women are often raped. It is a horrible way of saying," We have control of your country because we control your women." This is the one time when sex is not done in silence or secrecy. Rape of the enemy's women is not seen as a sex act but as an act of control.

As long as society views the sex act as something to be done in secret and in isolation, date rape will continue to occur. Because of the secrecy surrounding sex, rape is also surrounded in secrecy. Rape is bad for it is forced sex against a person's will. However, it is not worst than murder. Yet our society will often give a rapist more prison time than a murderer. Something is wrong with a society that considers rape worst than murder. Our society views sex as more valuable than life. In our society, a man will get more prison time for taking sex from a woman than for taking her life. This will continue as long as sex is viewed as a secret act rather than a private one.

Prostitution

Your mama was wrong about prostitution. If a person is sexually active with many different partners he or she is said to be promiscuous. If the person is sexually active with many different partners for money, he or she is said to be a prostitute. What makes a person a prostitute? Is it the act of performing sex or the act of performing sex for money? What is the difference between performing sex for fun and performing sex for money? What is a person called who performs sex for reasons other than love? Money is only one of the many reasons that a person has sex. A person may have sex for revenge, for power, for control, for self-esteem, and of course for love. An individual who is married may have sex for reasons other than love. He or she may continue to have sex long after love has stopped.

In our society prostitution is looked upon as an illegal and dishonorable profession. It is a crime in all but one of the fifty states. How is it that something as pleasurable and as healthy as sex can be looked upon as a crime? There is something wrong with a society where it is legal to sale alcohol and cigarettes -which are known to cause suffering and death but is illegal to sale sex. This is not to say that prostitution should be legalized but to question which one is more harmful. Society should question the basis for every law that deals with morality. It should determine if the laws deprive individuals of their right to choose how they will live their lives. Far too often society uses comfort as a standard for morality. Just because something is uncomfortable does not mean it is harmful or dangerous. If what an adult chooses to do is not dangerous or harmful and does not deprive another adult of the freedom of choice, does anyone or any society have the right to force that person to choose right? Freedom of choice means freedom to choose right or wrong. There is nothing wrong with speaking out against behaviors that are considered morally wrong. However, the line is crossed when laws are passed that force people to choose right. People have the right to choose wrong.

At its basic level prostitution is just sex. Sex is necessary for all living creatures. Humans are the only creatures that are prostitutes. They are the only ones that have sex for money. To put it another way, "only humans can be prostitutes". They are the only creatures that perform sex for money. Prostitution is a natural part of being human. Sex is not limited to humans but prostitution is. As long as there are humans who are not sexually satisfied there will be prostitutes who will fulfill those desires. As long as there is a demand there will be a supply. The reason prostitutes can not be eliminated is because they will do for money what wives will not do for love. Wives often have conditions for sex. Prostitutes have only one condition-money. The negative attitude that wives have about sexual variety is what keeps prostitutes in business. Husbands are prostitutes number one client .The number one sex act requested is oral sex. This is because orgasm by oral sex is probably the most enjoyable feeling known to humans. Both men and women enjoy oral sex. Many men would rather have oral sex than intercourse. Contrary to what many women have been taught, men do not want to "get in your pants" Because prostitutes know this, they remain successful. When a man gets with a prostitute, he is guaranteed to have sex. There is no such guarantee of sex with his wife. He may or may not have sex. The husbands who can not deal with this uncertainty may seek a prostitute. It is said that over fifty percent of marriages will have an affair. It is a good bet that the sex in the affair will be different from the sex in the marriage. People do not go seeking what they already have. Prostitution will continue as long as couples do not have unconditional sex in a loving relationship. Prostitutes may trade sex for money but there are people who trade sex for many other things. Prostitution is often narrowly defined as a sex act that is performed for money. However, prostitution can be defined as any act that is done solely for money and not love.

Abortion

Your mama was wrong about abortion. The question about abortion is not about when life begins. Those who argue that life begins at conception must not believe that the sperm and egg are alive. If they are alive then life must begin before conception. It is obvious that the sperm and egg are alive- for life can only come from life. Life must have started at some infinite time in the past. The argument, then, is not when does life begin but when does a person begin? Is a fertilized egg a live person? What is a live person? These questions will never be resolved. If conception begins a live person then why isn't an unborn child considered a dependent for tax purposes?

If a person kills a woman and her unborn child, society may charge the killer with double murder. For criminal purposes an unborn child is considered a person with rights. For tax purposes an unborn child is not considered a person. If an unborn child is a person, then the pregnant mother should be charged with child abuse if she does anything that would harm her unborn child.

Should an aborted fetus receive a burial? If it is a person, the answer is yes. Should a pregnant mother take out a life insurance policy to cover the burial cost in case of abortion? It is easy to see how this could become ridiculous. If the unborn child was treated the same as a person with all the rights of the born child, society would have to do a lot of unreasonable things.

In our society we believe that life ends when brain activity ends. Life therefore must begin when brain activity begins. Can there be brain activity if there is no brain? Can there be nerve activity without brain activity?

It is a known fact that there can be spontaneous movements of the limbs of a person after he or she has been pronounced brain dead.

It is not necessary to write volumes of books about abortion or any other subject. Common sense can solve most problems. Whatever position an individual holds it should be supported by facts that are consistent. If a person believes that an unborn child is a person, then the child should be a dependent for tax purposes. If the unborn child is not independent, then it is dependent. On the other hand if an individual believes that an unborn child is not a person, then a pregnant woman or any other person could not be charged with harm or abuse of the "non-person". How can anyone harm someone who does not exist?

The debate about abortion would be raised to another level if society would argue for tax deductions for the unborn child. It would seem to be the logical thing to do. If an unborn child is a dependent for moral purposes, then it should be a dependent for tax purposes. It's just common sense. Perhaps it is not about morality at all, but money.

About the Author

Dennis O. Evans is a 1969 graduate of Loma Linda University. After 25 years of teaching Music and English in both public and private schools, he retired in 1994 from the Bakersfield City School District in Bakersfield, California.

Since his retirement, he and his wife, Mary, have visited 44 states and lived in 4. He now lives in Loma Linda, California where he writes and works part-time as a substitute teacher. He and his wife love traveling, music, reading, art, and sports.

Printed in the United States
By Bookmasters